MW01039870

THE
ROTISSERIE
CHICKEN
COOKBOOK

Special thanks to our rotisserie chicken connoisseurs, Mel & Patrice. Without their creativity, this book would not exist!

THE ROTISSERIE CHICKEN COOKBOOK

13-Digit ISBN: 978-1-60433-991-8

10-Digit ISBN: 1-60433-991-8

This book may be ordered by mail from the publisher. Please include $5.99 for postage and handling. Please support your local bookseller first!

Books published by Cider Mill Press Book Publishers are available at special discounts for bulk purchases in the United States by corporations, institutions, and other organizations. For more information, please contact the publisher.

Cider Mill Press Book Publishers
"Where good books are ready for press"
PO Box 454
12 Spring Street
Kennebunkport, Maine 04046

Visit us online!
cidermillpress.com

Typography: Goodlife Sans Condensed, Skippy Sharp

Printed in China
1 2 3 4 5 6 7 8 9 0

First Edition

THE
ROTISSERIE
CHICKEN

COOKBOOK

Buy the Bird, Make 50 Quick Dishes

Illustrated by Michelle Xu

CIDER MILL
PRESS

BOOK
PUBLISHERS
KENNEBUNKPORT, MAINE

CONTENTS

Introduction 6

Sandwiches, Tacos & Other Favorites 10

Salads & Bowls 42

Soups 90

Index 121

INTRODUCTION

It's not too big of an overstatement to say that Boston Market introducing the take-home rotisserie chicken in the early '90s changed everything for the home cook. A massive hit right off the bat, it only took a few years for chains like Costco and Kroger to copy the bright idea, and soon every self-respecting grocery store had them ready to go, no matter the time of day. Considering that Americans purchased more than 600 million rotisserie chickens in 2017, it's clear many are grateful for that development.

Taking the price, convenience, nutrition, and, of course, exceptional flavor into account, that amount of birds flying off the store shelves is not surprising, albeit staggering. With time and energy increasingly at a premium, the possibility of swinging by the store, picking up a freshly cooked, succulent chicken (for less money than an uncooked bird), and having a wholesome, delicious centerpiece to a meal ready to go is a godsend. Simply slice, put it next to a few sides, and the feast can commence. And, usually, there's enough chicken left to form the basis of the next day's lunch, or another dinner.

But that simplicity and ease mean that one can go to the well once too often. Sliced rotisserie chicken breast beside a steamed or roasted vegetable is an amazing dinner considering how easy and affordable it is, but all food can become unappealing when repeated too frequently.

This is where *The Rotisserie Chicken Cookbook* swoops in to save the day, providing you with sandwiches, wraps, salads, bowls, and soups that retain the effortless character you love about these beautiful birds while providing a variety of flavors and textures to ensure that you can always keep things fresh. The rotisserie chicken lightened your load in the kitchen considerably—now it's time to spread your wings.

SANDWICHES, TACOS & OTHER FAVORITES

Slicing a rotisserie chicken and tossing it between two pieces of bread, in a tortilla, or on top of a pizza is one of the easiest indulgences you will ever come across. From a classic chicken salad to chipotle-laced chicken enchiladas, the preparations in this chapter are where you'll turn when it's time for a quick treat.

CLASSIC CHICKEN SALAD SANDWICHES

Yield: 4 to 6 Servings
Active Time: 5 Minutes / Total Time: 5 Minutes

This is the basic recipe beloved by many, but feel free to be bold with additions such as seedless grapes or mandarin oranges.

Ingredients

⅓ cup mayonnaise

½ cup chopped celery

1 shallot, chopped

1 teaspoon mustard

½ teaspoon fresh lemon juice

4 cups shredded or diced rotisserie chicken

¼ cup walnuts or pecans

Salt and pepper, to taste

Slices of sourdough bread, for serving

1. Place the mayonnaise, celery, shallot, mustard, and lemon juice in a mixing bowl and stir to combine.

2. Add the chicken and nuts and stir to incorporate. Season with salt and pepper and serve on the slices of sourdough.

PB & C SANDWICHES

Yield: 4 Servings

Active Time: 5 Minutes / Total Time: 5 Minutes

Before you turn your nose up at the thought of this, think of how well
Thai cuisine utilizes the trio of chicken, peanuts, and basil.

Ingredients

¼ cup smooth peanut butter

8 slices of sourdough bread

1½ cups shredded rotisserie chicken

¼ cup shredded fresh basil

½ teaspoon kosher salt

1. Spread the peanut butter over four slices of the bread. Top these slices with the chicken, basil, and salt and assemble the sandwiches using the remaining slices of bread.

BBQ CHICKEN SANDWICHES

Yield: 4 to 6 Servings

Active Time: 5 Minutes / Total Time: 5 Minutes

If your local grocery store is one of those that sells seasoned rotisserie chickens, these BBQ sandwiches are a good spot to try out the spicy-leaning offerings.

Ingredients

3 tablespoons mayonnaise, plus more to taste

1 tablespoon apple cider vinegar

¼ yellow onion, minced

2 tablespoons finely chopped fresh chives

2 cups shredded napa cabbage

Salt and pepper, to taste

2 to 3 cups shredded rotisserie chicken

½ cup barbecue sauce

4 to 6 brioche buns

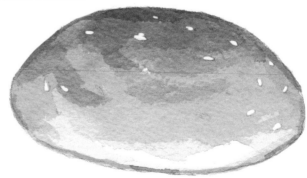

1. Place the mayonnaise, apple cider vinegar, onion, chives, and cabbage in a mixing bowl and stir to combine. Season with salt and pepper, add additional mayonnaise if desired, and set the slaw aside.

2. Place the chicken and barbecue sauce in a mixing bowl and stir to combine.

3. Spread some mayonnaise on the top halves of the brioche buns and set them aside. Place the chicken on the bottom halves of the buns and top with some of the slaw. Assemble the sandwiches and serve.

CHICKEN PANINIS WITH SUN-DRIED TOMATO AIOLI

Yield: 4 Servings

Active Time: 10 Minutes / Total Time: 10 Minutes

Constructing a memorable sandwich starts with quality bread—though a sun-dried tomato aioli doesn't hurt.

Ingredients

For the Aioli

1 cup chopped sun-dried tomatoes

1 cup mayonnaise

1 tablespoon whole grain mustard

2 tablespoons finely chopped fresh parsley

2 tablespoons minced scallions

1 teaspoon white balsamic vinegar

1 garlic clove, minced

2 teaspoons kosher salt

1 teaspoon black pepper

For the Sandwiches

8 slices of crusty bread

8 slices of cheddar cheese

Breasts from 2 rotisserie chickens, sliced

12 slices of cooked bacon

1 cup arugula

1. Preheat a panini press. To prepare the aioli, place all of the ingredients in a mixing bowl and stir until combined.

2. To begin preparations for the sandwiches, spread some of the aioli on each slice of bread. Place a slice of cheddar on each slice of bread. Divide the chicken between four pieces of the bread.

Top each portion of chicken with 3 slices of bacon and ¼ cup of the arugula and then assemble the sandwiches.

3. Place the sandwiches in the panini press and press until the cheese has melted and there is a nice crust on the bread. Remove and serve immediately.

Note: If you don't have a panini press, don't worry. Simply place 1 tablespoon of olive oil in a large skillet and warm over medium–high heat. Place a sandwich in the pan, place a warmed cast–iron skillet on top so it is pressing down on the sandwich, and cook until golden brown. Turn the sandwich over and repeat.

CHICKEN BURRITOS

Yield: 6 Servings

Active Time: 20 Minutes / Total Time: 30 Minutes

A great, quick weeknight dinner, or filling, flavor-packed lunches for an entire workweek.

Ingredients

1 cup white or brown rice

¼ cup finely chopped fresh cilantro

1 large yellow squash, cut into long slices

1 large zucchini, cut into long slices

2 ears of corn, shucked

1 tablespoon olive oil

1 (14 oz.) can black beans

3 cups shredded rotisserie chicken

1 small red onion, chopped

2 tomatoes, diced

1 cup grated pepper jack cheese

6 large flour tortillas

Salsa, for serving

Sour cream, for serving

1. Cook the rice according to the instructions on the package. Once it has cooked completely, transfer it to a bowl, stir in the cilantro, and set aside.

2. While the rice is cooking, preheat your grill to 450°F. Brush the squash, zucchini, and corn with olive oil. Place the vegetables on the grill and cook, turning occasionally, until they are charred and tender, about 10 minutes. Remove from heat and dice the zucchini and squash. Remove the corn kernels from the cobs and discard the cobs. Place the grilled vegetables in a bowl. Leave the grill on.

3. While the vegetables are grilling, drain and rinse the black beans. If desired, warm them in a saucepan.

4. Layer the rice-and-cilantro mixture, beans, chicken, grilled veggies, onion, tomatoes, and cheese on the tortillas. Wrap tightly, grill for about 1 minute per side, and serve immediately with salsa and sour cream.

CHICKEN FAJITAS

Yield: 6 Servings

Active Time: 20 Minutes / Total Time: 35 Minutes

The trick is to bring this dish to the table while the meat and veggies are still sizzling, as the sound is sure to get mouths watering.

Ingredients

For the Chicken

½ cup orange juice

Juice of 1 lime

4 garlic cloves, minced

1 jalapeño pepper, stemmed, seeded, and minced

2 tablespoons finely chopped fresh cilantro

1 teaspoon cumin

1 teaspoon dried oregano

Salt and pepper, to taste

3 tablespoons olive oil

Breasts from 2 rotisserie chickens, sliced

For the Vegetables

2 tablespoons olive oil

1 red onion, sliced thin

3 bell peppers, stemmed, seeded, and sliced thin

2 jalapeño peppers, stemmed, seeded, and sliced thin

3 garlic cloves, minced

¼ cup fresh lime juice

½ cup finely chopped fresh cilantro

Salt and pepper, to taste

Corn tortillas, for serving

Guacamole, for serving

Salsa, for serving

1. To begin preparations for the chicken, place the orange juice, lime juice, garlic, jalapeño, cilantro, cumin, oregano, salt, and pepper in a bowl and stir to combine. When thoroughly combined, add the olive oil.

2. Add the chicken pieces to the mixture, stir until they are evenly coated, cover with plastic wrap, and let stand for 15 minutes.

3. To prepare the vegetables, place the olive oil in a 12-inch cast-iron skillet and warm over medium heat. When the oil starts to shimmer, add the onion, peppers, and garlic. Cook, while stirring, until the vegetables have softened, about 5 minutes. Add the lime juice and cilantro, season with salt and pepper, and cook until the vegetables are tender, about 10 minutes.

4. Push the vegetables to one side of the pan and put the chicken on the other side. Cook, while stirring, until the chicken is warmed through. Serve immediately with corn tortillas, guacamole, and salsa.

CHICKEN TACOS

Yield: 6 Servings

Active Time: 10 Minutes / Total Time: 1 Hour

The beauty of the rotisserie chicken becomes clear when you realize this beloved dish is no more than 10 minutes of labor away.

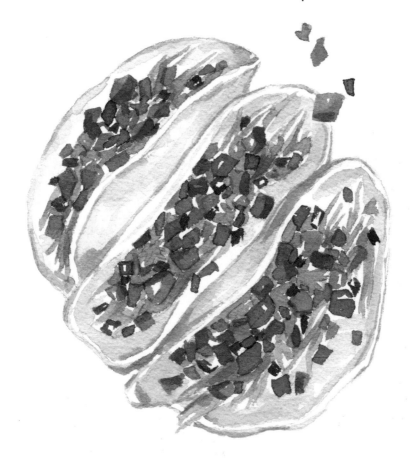

Ingredients

For the Pico de Gallo

4 plum tomatoes, diced

1 jalapeño pepper, stemmed, seeded, and diced

½ cup chopped red onion

¼ cup finely chopped fresh cilantro

Zest and juice of ½ lime

Salt, to taste

For the Tacos

4 cups shredded rotisserie chicken

1 tablespoon kosher salt

1 tablespoon cumin

1 tablespoon garlic powder

1 tablespoon cayenne pepper

Adobo sauce, to taste

Hard taco shells or corn tortillas, for serving

1. To prepare the pico de gallo, place all of the ingredients in a mixing bowl and stir to combine. Refrigerate for 1 hour before serving to let the flavors mingle.

2. To prepare the tacos, place all of the ingredients, except for the taco shells or tortillas, in a mixing bowl and toss to combine.

3. If desired, warm the dressed chicken in a skillet for 1 or 2 minutes. Place the chicken in the taco shells or tortillas and serve alongside the pico de gallo and other preferred fixings.

CHICKEN TOSTADAS WITH CILANTRO-LIME SOUR CREAM

Yield: 4 Servings
Active Time: 20 Minutes / Total Time: 25 Minutes

For those evenings when you need to bring a little bit more to the table, but are still craving tacos.

Ingredients

For the Tostadas

½ cup corn kernels

1 small jalapeño pepper, stemmed, seeded, and chopped, plus more for garnish

¼ cup minced red onion

1 garlic clove, minced

1½ tablespoons fresh lime juice

¼ cup finely chopped cilantro, plus more for garnish

½ cup chopped tomato

Salt and pepper, to taste

2 cups vegetable oil

8 corn tortillas

Paprika, to taste

4 cups chopped or shredded rotisserie chicken

Red cabbage, shredded, for garnish

Lime wedges, for serving

For the Sour Cream

½ cup finely chopped fresh cilantro

¼ cup fresh lime juice

1¼ cups sour cream

1½ teaspoons kosher salt

½ teaspoon black pepper

1. To begin preparations for the tostadas, place the corn, jalapeño, onion, garlic, lime juice, cilantro, and tomato in a mixing bowl and stir to combine. Season with salt and pepper and set aside.

2. To prepare the sour cream, place all of the ingredients in a mixing bowl, stir to combine, and set aside.

3. Place the oil in a Dutch oven and warm to 350°F over medium-high heat. Working with one tortilla at a time, place it in the oil and fry until crispy.

4. Remove from the oil, transfer to a paper towel–lined plate, and season with salt and paprika.

5. Spread some sour cream on each tortilla and top with the corn salsa and chicken. Garnish with red cabbage and additional jalapeño and cilantro and serve with the lime wedges.

CHIPOTLE CHICKEN ENCHILADAS

Yield: 4 to 6 Servings
Active Time: 25 Minutes / Total Time: 1 Hour and 20 Minutes

Chipotles are smoked jalapeño peppers. The smoking tempers the heat just enough that the smoke and sweetness can step forward.

Ingredients

For the Sauce

4 dried chipotle peppers

½ (7 oz.) can diced mild green chilies

2 tablespoons olive oil

2 to 3 plum tomatoes, seeded

1 tablespoon tomato paste

1 tablespoon cumin

1 teaspoon dried oregano

Salt and pepper, to taste

For the Enchiladas

2 tablespoons olive oil

1 to 2 russet potatoes, peeled and minced

½ white onion, minced

2 garlic cloves, minced

3 cups shredded rotisserie chicken

Salt and pepper, to taste

1 cup chicken stock (see pages 92-93 for homemade)

½ (7 oz.) can diced mild green chilies

16 to 24 corn tortillas

1 cup crumbled Cotija cheese, for garnish

Fresh cilantro, finely chopped, for garnish

1. To prepare the sauce, bring water to a boil in a small saucepan. Add the chipotles and cook until reconstituted, about 10 minutes. Drain and transfer the chipotles to a blender or food processor. Add the remaining ingredients and puree until smooth. Add the puree to the saucepan and cook over medium–low heat until the sauce is thick enough to coat the back of a spoon, about 15 minutes. Remove the sauce from the pan and set aside.

2. To begin preparations for the enchiladas, place the oil in a cast–iron skillet and warm over medium–high heat. When it starts to shimmer, add the potatoes and cook, stirring occasionally, until they start to soften, about 5 minutes.

3. Add the onion and garlic and cook until the onion starts to soften, about 4 minutes.

4. Reduce the heat to medium and add the shredded chicken, salt and pepper, the stock, the green chilies, and 1 tablespoon of the sauce. Cook until the stock has evaporated, about 5 minutes. Remove the mixture from the pan and set it aside.

5. Preheat the oven to 375°F and grease a 9 x 13–inch baking pan with nonstick cooking spray. Place the tortillas on a work surface and spread a small amount of sauce on each of them. Evenly distribute the filling between the tortillas and roll them up. Place the filled tortillas in the baking pan, seam–side down.

6. Top the enchiladas with the remaining sauce and place the pan in the oven. Bake for 20 minutes, or until a crust forms on the exterior of the tortillas. Garnish with the Cotija cheese and cilantro and serve.

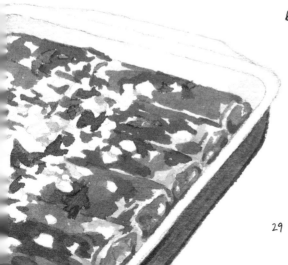

CHICKEN & TOMATILLO CASSEROLE

Yield: 6 Servings

Active Time: 15 Minutes / Total Time: 1 Hour

Packed with shredded chicken and tangy tomatillos, this is what lasagna might have been had it been created in the American Southwest.

Ingredients

2 tomatillos, husked, rinsed, and halved

1 plum tomato, halved

2 garlic cloves

1 shallot, halved

1 poblano pepper, stemmed, seeded, and halved

¼ cup olive oil

1 tablespoon kosher salt, plus 1 pinch

1 tablespoon cumin

4 cups shredded rotisserie chicken

2 eggs, beaten

1 (14 oz.) can fire-roasted tomatoes

14 corn tortillas

1 cup salsa verde

¼ cup crumbled Cotija cheese

1. Place the tomatillos, fresh tomato, garlic, shallot, poblano pepper, olive oil, salt, and cumin in a blender and puree until smooth. Place the chicken in a large mixing bowl, pour the puree over the chicken, and stir to combine. Let stand for 15 minutes.

2. Preheat the oven to 375°F. Add the eggs, canned tomatoes, and remaining salt to the mixing bowl containing the chicken mixture and stir to combine.

3. Place four of the tortillas in a square 8-inch baking dish. Add half of the chicken mixture, top with four more tortillas, and add the remaining chicken mixture. Top with the remaining tortillas, cover with the salsa verde, and then place the dish in the oven. Bake for about 30 minutes, until the center is hot. Remove, sprinkle the cheese on top, and return to the oven. Bake until the cheese has melted, remove, and serve.

CHICKEN & KIMCHI POT STICKERS

Yield: 4 Servings
Active Time: 30 Minutes / Total Time: 1 Hour

Legend has it that these dumplings are the result of a chef forgetting that they were in the wok, an accident that gave them a delightful crispy and golden burnish.

Ingredients

2 cups ground rotisserie chicken

1 cup kimchi, minced

1 tablespoon soy sauce

3-inch piece fresh ginger, peeled and minced

1½ teaspoons toasted sesame oil

1½ teaspoons Shaoxing rice wine

1½ teaspoons sugar

1 garlic clove, minced

1 scallion, trimmed and minced

1 tablespoon cornstarch

30 wonton wrappers

3 tablespoons peanut oil

Chili garlic sauce, for serving

1. Place the chicken, kimchi, soy sauce, ginger, sesame oil, rice wine, sugar, garlic, and scallion in a mixing bowl and stir until well combined. Sprinkle the cornstarch over the top and stir to incorporate. Cover with plastic wrap and let sit for 30 minutes.

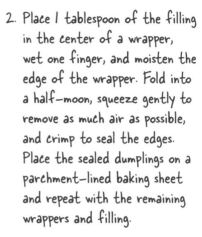

2. Place 1 tablespoon of the filling in the center of a wrapper, wet one finger, and moisten the edge of the wrapper. Fold into a half-moon, squeeze gently to remove as much air as possible, and crimp to seal the edges. Place the sealed dumplings on a parchment-lined baking sheet and repeat with the remaining wrappers and filling.

3. Place 1 tablespoon of the peanut oil in a large skillet and warm over medium-high heat. When it starts to shimmer, add the dumplings in batches and cook until they are golden brown on the bottom. Add a few tablespoons of water, cover, and steam until cooked through, about 4 minutes. Transfer the cooked dumplings to a warmed platter and tent with aluminum foil to keep warm. Dry the skillet with a paper towel and repeat until all of the dumplings have been cooked. Serve alongside the chili garlic sauce.

CHICKEN & MUSHROOM CREPES

Yield: 6 Servings
Active Time: 40 Minutes / Total Time: 4 Hours

Sure, crepes are a bit time-and-labor intensive. But since the rotisserie chicken saved you some of each, this dish is a worthy spot for reinvestment.

Ingredients

For the Crepes

4 tablespoons unsalted butter

3 eggs

Pinch of kosher salt

1 cup whole milk, plus more as needed

14 tablespoons all-purpose flour

For the Filling

4 tablespoons unsalted butter

1 lb. mushrooms, chopped

3 cups diced rotisserie chicken

1 (14 oz.) can cream of mushroom soup

2 tablespoons vermouth

⅓ cup whole milk

2 tablespoons finely chopped fresh parsley

Salt and pepper, to taste

1. To begin preparations for the crepes, place a 12-inch cast-iron skillet over low heat and melt 2 tablespoons of the butter in it. Place the eggs in a mixing bowl and scramble. Add the salt and milk to the eggs and whisk to incorporate. Incorporate the flour and melted butter and whisk until the batter is smooth and contains no lumps. Cover the bowl with plastic wrap, put it in a cool, dark place, and let it rest for 3 hours.

2. To prepare the filling, place the butter in the skillet and melt over medium heat. Add the mushrooms and cook, stirring frequently, until they start to brown, about 6 minutes. Stir in the chicken, cream of mushroom soup, vermouth, milk, and parsley and cook until warmed through, about 3 minutes. Season with salt and pepper, transfer the mixture to a bowl, and set aside.

3. Wipe out the skillet, place it over medium-high heat, and melt a slice of the remaining butter in it. When the skillet is hot but not smoking, scoop about ¼ cup of batter into the skillet. When the batter hits the pan, gently tilt the skillet to spread the batter evenly over the bottom. When the bottom is covered, cook until the edge of the crepe starts to lift up, about 1 minute. Flip the crepe over and cook the other side for about half as long. Tilt the skillet over a plate to slide the crepe out. Repeat with the remaining crepe batter, adding butter when the pan starts to look dry. Separate the cooked crepes with pieces of parchment paper.

4. Preheat the oven to 350°F and grease a 9 x 13-inch baking dish. Working with one crepe at a time, put a generous scoop of the filling in the middle and fold the crepe around the filling. Place the filled crepes in the baking dish, seam-side down. Cover the filled baking dish with aluminum foil and bake for about 30 minutes, until the filling is bubbling and hot. Remove from the oven, remove the foil, and let the crepes cool for a few minutes before serving.

CHICKEN PARMESAN CALZONES

Yield: 4 Servings

Active Time: 20 Minutes / Total Time: 1 Hour

"00" flour is a very finely milled white flour and essential for producing restaurant-quality pizza and calzones at home.

Ingredients

1 cup warm water (104 to 112°F)

1 tablespoon active dry yeast

1 tablespoon sugar

1 tablespoon olive oil

2½ cups "00" or all-purpose flour, plus more for dusting

1 teaspoon kosher salt

3 cups shredded rotisserie chicken

¾ cup grated Parmesan cheese, plus more for topping

1 cup marinara sauce

½ lb. fresh mozzarella cheese, sliced

1. Preheat the oven to 450°F. Place the water, yeast, and sugar in a large mixing bowl and stir gently. Let the mixture sit until it begins to bubble, 7 to 10 minutes.

2. Add the olive oil to the mixture and stir. Add the flour and salt and stir until the dough starts to hold together.

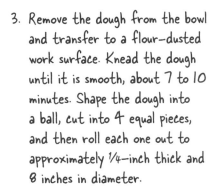

3. Remove the dough from the bowl and transfer to a flour-dusted work surface. Knead the dough until it is smooth, about 7 to 10 minutes. Shape the dough into a ball, cut into 4 equal pieces, and then roll each one out to approximately ¼-inch thick and 8 inches in diameter.

4. Place the chicken and Parmesan in a bowl and toss to combine. Divide the mixture evenly between the pieces of dough. Top with some of the marinara sauce and mozzarella, fold the dough over itself to form pockets, and crimp the edges to seal.

5. Place the calzones on parchment-lined baking sheets, sprinkle additional Parmesan on top, and poke a few holes in the top of each calzone. Place the calzones in the oven and bake for 20 to 25 minutes, until the calzones are golden brown. Remove from the oven and let rest for 10 minutes before serving.

BBQ CHICKEN PIZZA

Yield: 4 Servings

Active Time: 20 Minutes / Total Time: 1 Hour

When selecting a barbecue sauce, it's better to look for one that leans more toward savory than sweet.

Ingredients

1 cup warm water (104 to 112°F)

1 tablespoon active dry yeast

1 tablespoon sugar

1 tablespoon olive oil

2½ cups "00" or all-purpose flour, plus more for dusting

1 teaspoon kosher salt

½ cup barbecue sauce

2 cups shredded rotisserie chicken

⅔ cup grated smoked gouda cheese

⅔ cup shredded mozzarella cheese

½ red onion, sliced thin

1. Preheat the oven to 450°F. Place the water, yeast, and sugar in a large mixing bowl and stir gently. Let the mixture sit until it begins to bubble, about 7 to 10 minutes.

2. Add the olive oil to the mixture and stir. Add the flour and salt and stir until a dough forms. Remove the dough from the bowl and transfer to a flour-dusted work surface. Knead the dough until it is smooth, about 7 to 10 minutes. Shape the dough into a ball and then roll out to desired shape.

3. Place the dough on a greased pan and use a fork to poke holes in the dough, which will prevent air pockets from forming. Place the dough on the lowest rack of your oven and bake for 5 to 7 minutes, until the dough starts to brown. Remove and raise the oven's temperature to 500°F.

4. Place 2 tablespoons of the barbecue sauce and the shredded chicken in a mixing bowl and stir until the chicken is evenly coated. Spread the rest of the barbecue sauce on the baked dough. Top with the dressed chicken, cheeses, and the red onion and place the pizza in the oven. Bake until the cheese is melted and browned and the crust is golden brown. Remove and let cool briefly before slicing and serving.

CHICKEN POT PIE

Yield: 6 Servings

Active Time: 20 Minutes / Total Time: 1 Hour

If you've got a little extra time, make multiple pies and freeze the extra ones for some future date.

Ingredients

2 piecrusts

2 tablespoons olive oil

½ yellow onion, chopped

1 garlic clove, minced

1 carrot, peeled and chopped

2 cups diced rotisserie chicken

¾ cup chopped green beans

2 tablespoons unsalted butter

2 tablespoons all-purpose flour

1¼ cups milk, at room temperature

Salt and pepper, to taste

1 tablespoon half-and-half

1. Preheat the oven to 350°F. Place one of the piecrusts in a greased 9-inch pie plate.

2. Place the olive oil in a small skillet and warm over medium heat. When it starts to shimmer, add the onion and garlic and cook, while stirring, until the onion turns translucent, about 3 minutes. Add the carrot, reduce the heat to low, cover the pan, and cook, stirring occasionally, until the carrot starts to soften and the onion starts to caramelize, about 5 minutes. Remove from heat and spread the mixture over the crust in the pie plate. Distribute the chicken and green beans on top.

3. Place the butter in a small saucepan and melt over medium heat. While stirring constantly, sprinkle the flour over the melted butter. Reduce heat to low and gradually add the milk. Stir until the sauce has thickened and reduced slightly, about 5 minutes.

4. Pour the sauce over the mixture in the crust and season with salt and pepper. Lay the remaining piecrust over the filling and crimp the edge to seal it. Cut three or four slits in the center of the top crust and brush it with the half-and-half.

5. Place the pie in the oven and bake for 30 to 40 minutes, until the crust is golden brown and the filling is bubbling. Remove from the oven and let cool slightly before serving.

SALADS
&
BOWLS

Combining a rotisserie chicken with another rapidly ready preparation—the salad—is a great move when you've got to get out the door. If you've got a little more time, and a hankering for something a little more substantial, the various rice and noodle bowls in the latter part of the chapter will meet your needs.

CHICKEN CAESAR SALAD

Yield: 4 to 6 Servings

Active Time: 5 Minutes / Total Time: 5 Minutes

Simple, delicious, and nutritious, this cornerstone of the contemporary diet was made for the advent of the rotisserie chicken.

Ingredients

2 garlic cloves, chopped

½ cup olive oil

2 to 4 anchovy fillets, chopped

2 tablespoons fresh lemon juice

Salt and pepper, to taste

4 romaine lettuce hearts, chopped

2 to 3 cups diced rotisserie chicken

4 slices of crusty bread, toasted and chopped

¾ cup grated Parmesan cheese

1. Place the garlic, olive oil, anchovy fillets, and lemon juice in a food processor or blender and puree until smooth. Season with salt and pepper and set the dressing aside.

2. Place the lettuce in a salad bowl, add 2 to 3 tablespoons of the dressing, and toss to combine. Add the chicken, bread, Parmesan, and remaining dressing, toss to combine, and serve.

RICE NOODLE SALAD

Yield: 6 Servings

Active Time: 40 Minutes / Total Time: 24 Hours

A salad that is perfect for those hot summer nights when you're terrified by the prospect of turning on the oven.

Ingredients

For the Peanut Sauce

¼ cup fresh lime juice

2-inch piece fresh ginger, peeled and minced

1 garlic clove

¼ cup brown sugar

2 tablespoons fish sauce

2 tablespoons soy sauce

½ cup smooth peanut butter

For the Salad

1 lb. rice stick noodles

½ lb. carrots, peeled and sliced thin

1 red bell pepper, stemmed, seeded, and sliced thin

1 Fresno chili pepper, stemmed, seeded, and sliced thin

2 jalapeño peppers, stemmed, seeded, and sliced thin

4 scallions, trimmed and sliced thin

1 cup fresh basil leaves

¼ cup finely chopped fresh cilantro

2 tablespoons finely chopped fresh mint

4 cups diced rotisserie chicken

¼ cup crushed peanuts

1. To prepare the peanut sauce, place all of the ingredients in a blender and puree until smooth. Transfer to the refrigerator and chill overnight.

2. To begin preparations for the salad, bring water to a boil in a large saucepan and add the noodles. Cook, while stirring, until the noodles are just tender, about 3 minutes. Drain, rinse with cold water, and set them aside so they can drain further.

3. Place the noodles and the remaining ingredients in a salad bowl. Stir to combine, add the peanut sauce, toss to coat, and serve.

CURRIED CHICKEN SALAD

Yield: 6 Servings

Active Time: 15 Minutes / Total Time: 45 Minutes

If you'd prefer to make sandwiches with this salad, toasted marble rye is the best bread option by far.

Ingredients

½ cup mayonnaise

3 tablespoons fresh lime juice

¼ cup Madras curry powder

1 tablespoon cumin

1 tablespoon granulated garlic

½ teaspoon cinnamon

½ teaspoon turmeric

2 cups minced celery

2 Granny Smith apples, minced

½ red bell pepper, stemmed, seeded, and minced

¾ cup chopped pecans

4 cups chopped rotisserie chicken

5 oz baby arugula

Salt and pepper, to taste

1. Place the mayonnaise, lime juice, and all of the seasonings in a salad bowl and stir to combine. Add the celery, apples, bell pepper, and ½ cup of the pecans and stir to incorporate.

2. Add the chicken and arugula to the bowl and toss to combine. Season with salt and pepper, top with the remaining pecans, and serve.

CAULIFLOWER & CHICKPEA SALAD

Yield: 4 Servings
Active Time: 25 Minutes / Total Time: 45 Minutes

Crunchy cauliflower, nutty chickpeas, and a perfect balance of sweet and spicy place this salad a notch above other dishes sharing that designation.

Ingredients

For the Salad

1 (14 oz.) can chickpeas, drained and rinsed

3 cups cauliflower florets

3 garlic cloves, sliced thin

1 shallot, sliced thin

⅓ cup olive oil

½ teaspoon dark chili powder

½ teaspoon chipotle powder

½ teaspoon black pepper

½ teaspoon onion powder

½ teaspoon garlic powder

¼ teaspoon paprika

1 tablespoon kosher salt

4 cups shredded or diced rotisserie chicken

For the Dressing

2 scallions, trimmed and sliced thin

2 Fresno chili peppers, stemmed, seeded, and sliced thin

3 tablespoons sugar

¼ cup red wine vinegar

½ teaspoon dark chili powder

½ teaspoon chipotle powder

½ teaspoon black pepper

½ teaspoon onion powder

½ teaspoon garlic powder

¼ teaspoon paprika

½ tablespoon kosher salt

1. Preheat the oven to 400°F. To begin preparations for the salad, place all of the ingredients, except for the chicken, in a mixing bowl and toss to combine. Place the mixture in a 9 x 13-inch baking pan, place the pan in the oven, and bake until the cauliflower is slightly charred and still crunchy, about 30 minutes. Let the mixture cool slightly while you prepare the dressing.

2. To prepare the dressing, place all of the ingredients in a salad bowl and stir until the sugar has dissolved.

3. Place the chicken and the cauliflower-and-chickpea mixture in the bowl, toss to combine, and serve.

LARB GAI

Yield: 4 Servings
Active Time: 20 Minutes / Total Time: 35 Minutes

If in glancing over the ingredients you hesitate over the toasted rice powder, don't worry—just toast ½ cup jasmine rice in a dry skillet until light brown and then grind it into a powder.

Ingredients

1 tablespoon olive oil

1 shallot, minced

3 cups ground rotisserie chicken

1 lemongrass stalk, minced

2 makrut lime leaves, minced

3 red chili peppers, stemmed, seeded, and chopped (optional)

¼ cup fresh lime juice

1 tablespoon fish sauce

1 tablespoon soy sauce

1 tablespoon toasted rice powder

¼ cup finely chopped fresh cilantro

12 fresh mint leaves, finely chopped

Salt and pepper, to taste

Bibb lettuce leaves, for serving

1. Place a skillet over medium heat and add the olive oil. When the oil starts to shimmer, add the shallot and cook until it turns translucent, about 3 minutes. Transfer to the bowl containing the ground chicken.

2. Add the lemongrass, lime leaves, chili peppers (if using), lime juice, fish sauce, soy sauce, toasted rice powder, cilantro, and mint to the bowl. Stir to combine, taste, and season with salt and pepper.

3. Serve with the lettuce leaves, using them to scoop up the mixture.

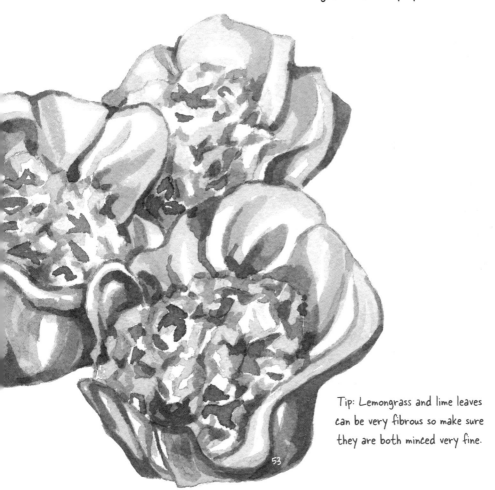

Tip: Lemongrass and lime leaves can be very fibrous so make sure they are both minced very fine.

CHICKEN RAMEN

Yield: 4 Servings

Active Time: 20 Minutes / Total Time: 30 Minutes

Comforting but not heavy, thanks to the miso-based broth. The vegetables are selected to provide balance, but you can substitute nearly anything you like.

Ingredients

1 tablespoon olive oil

1 cup fresh shiitake mushrooms, stems removed, chopped

4 cups chicken stock (see pages 92–93 for homemade)

1-inch piece fresh ginger, peeled and minced

4 oz bok choy, trimmed and sliced

1½ cups chopped asparagus

4 oz ramen noodles

2 radishes, sliced

1 tablespoon white miso paste

2 tablespoons soy sauce

2 tablespoons mirin

3 cups shredded or diced rotisserie chicken

1. Place the oil in a medium saucepan and warm over medium heat. When the oil starts to shimmer, add the shiitakes and cook, turning occasionally, until browned all over, about 10 minutes. Remove the mushrooms from the pan and transfer them to a bowl.

2. Add the stock and ginger to the pan and bring to a simmer. Add all of the remaining ingredients, except for the chicken. Stir to combine and simmer until the noodles and vegetables are cooked through, 5 to 8 minutes.

3. Add the chicken and return the mushrooms to the pan, stir to incorporate, and cook until warmed through. Taste, adjust seasoning as needed, and ladle into warmed bowls.

GARDEN SESAME NOODLES

Yield: 6 Servings

Active Time: 15 Minutes / Total Time: 30 Minutes

Noodles seasoned with this sesame sauce can take on just about anything. By pairing leftover chicken with the bounty of a summer garden, you're about to see just how true that is.

Ingredients

1 lb. Chinese egg noodles

2½ tablespoons toasted sesame oil

2 tablespoons tahini

1½ tablespoons smooth peanut butter

¼ cup soy sauce

2 tablespoons rice vinegar

1 tablespoon light brown sugar

2 teaspoons chili garlic sauce, plus more for serving

2-inch piece fresh ginger, peeled and minced

2 garlic cloves, minced

1 yellow or orange bell pepper, stemmed, seeded, and sliced thin

2 cups diced rotisserie chicken

1 cucumber, peeled, seeded, and sliced thin

1 cup snow peas, trimmed

½ cup chopped roasted peanuts

2 tablespoons sesame seeds, toasted

6 scallions, trimmed and chopped

1. Bring a large pot of water to a boil. Add the noodles and stir for the first minute to prevent any sticking. Cook until tender but still chewy, 2 to 3 minutes. Drain and transfer the noodles to a large bowl. Add ½ tablespoon of the sesame oil and toss to coat to prevent the noodles from sticking together.

2. Place the tahini and peanut butter in a small bowl. Add the soy sauce, vinegar, the remaining sesame oil, the sugar, chili garlic sauce, ginger, and garlic and whisk until combined. Taste and adjust the seasoning as needed.

3. Add the sauce to the noodles and toss until coated. Arrange the noodles in six bowls and top with the pepper, chicken, cucumber, snow peas, peanuts, sesame seeds, and scallions. Serve with additional chili garlic sauce.

PUERTO RICAN RICE & BEANS

Yield: 6 Servings

Active Time: 15 Minutes / Total Time: 24 Hours

An authentic recipe utilizes kidney beans, but black beans will also work if that's your preference.

Ingredients

½ lb. kidney beans, soaked overnight and drained

½ cup olive oil

½ cup minced salt pork

2 cups Spanish-style tomato sauce, pureed

2 cups white rice

3 cups chicken stock (see pages 92–93 for homemade)

2 packets Sazón with achiote

2 tablespoons dried oregano

1 cup Spanish olives with brine

Adobo seasoning, to taste

3 cups shredded rotisserie chicken

Salt and pepper, to taste

1. Place the beans in a Dutch oven and cover with water. Bring to a boil, reduce the heat to medium-low, and cover the pot. Cook until the beans are tender, 45 minutes to 1 hour. Drain and set the beans aside.

2. Add the salt pork and the remaining oil to the pot and cook until the salt pork's fat has rendered, about 5 minutes. Add the tomato sauce and cook for 5 minutes, while stirring constantly.

3. Add the rice to the pot, stir, and cook for 5 minutes. Add all of the remaining ingredients, except for the chicken, raise heat to medium, and cook for 10 minutes. Cover the Dutch oven and cook until the liquid has been absorbed and the rice is tender, 20 to 30 minutes. Uncover the pot, stir in the chicken and beans, season with salt and pepper, and serve.

BUDDHA SESAME CHICKEN

Yield: 4 to 6 Servings

Active Time: 35 Minutes / Total Time: 45 Minutes

A meal worthy of a big night out on the town, all in the comfort of your own home.

Ingredients

For the Sauce

½ cup water, plus more as needed

⅓ cup sugar

¼ cup mushroom soy sauce

½ cup soy sauce

¼ cup white wine vinegar

2 garlic cloves, minced

1-inch piece fresh ginger, peeled and minced

For the Chicken

⅓ cup vegetable oil, plus more as needed

⅓ cup cornstarch

Breasts from 2 rotisserie chickens, sliced

½ lb. mushrooms, trimmed and quartered

1 shallot, minced

1 lb. asparagus, trimmed and cut into 3-inch pieces

For Garnish

Sesame seeds

For Serving

Cooked white or brown rice

1. To prepare the sauce, place all of the ingredients in a bowl and whisk to combine. Set the sauce aside.

2. To begin preparations for the chicken, place the oil in a small bowl and gradually add the cornstarch, stirring constantly to prevent lumps from forming.

3. Add vegetable oil to a Dutch oven until it is about 3 inches deep and heat to 350°F. Dredge the chicken in the cornstarch mixture until completely coated. Working in batches, gently drop the chicken in the oil and fry until golden brown, about 3 minutes. Transfer the cooked strips to a paper towel–lined plate. Set the cornstarch mixture aside; you will use it to thicken the sauce later on.

4. Place a small amount of oil in a large skillet and warm over medium heat. Add the mushrooms, making sure they are in one layer, and cook until they are browned all over, about 10 minutes. Transfer the mushrooms to a bowl, add the shallot to the pan, and sauté until fragrant, about 1 minute. Add the asparagus and cook until it starts to brown, about 4 minutes. Transfer the shallot and asparagus to the bowl containing the mushrooms.

5. Pour the sauce into the pan and scrape up any browned bits that are stuck to the bottom of the skillet. Bring to a boil, add a teaspoon of the cornstarch mixture, and stir until the sauce has thickened. If it does not thicken enough, add another teaspoon. If it is too thick, add a little water. When the sauce has reached the desired consistency, return the chicken and vegetables to the pan and toss to coat. Garnish with sesame seeds and serve over rice.

BBQ CHICKEN HASH

Yield: 4 to 6 Servings

Active Time: 40 Minutes / Total Time: 1 Hour and 30 Minutes

With fried eggs or by itself, this hash provides comfort morning, noon, and night.

Ingredients

2 large russet potatoes, peeled and chopped

1 teaspoon kosher salt, plus more to taste

3 tablespoons unsalted butter

1 Vidalia onion, chopped

3 garlic cloves, minced

1 small jalapeño pepper, stemmed, seeded, and sliced

4 cups shredded rotisserie chicken

1/4 cup barbecue sauce

Black pepper, to taste

Salsa, for serving

Sour cream, for serving

1. Place the potatoes in a saucepan and cover with cold water. Add the teaspoon of salt. Bring to a boil, reduce the heat to medium, and cook the potatoes for about 10 minutes. You don't want to cook them until they are tender, as this will cause them to fall apart in the hash. Drain, rinse with cold water, and let the potatoes drain further.

2. Melt the butter in a large cast-iron skillet. Add the onion, garlic, and jalapeño and cook over medium-high heat, while stirring, until the vegetables start to soften, about 5 minutes.

3. Add the potatoes and press them down into the skillet. Cook without disturbing them for about 5 minutes, then start turning sections over with a spatula while stirring in the chicken and the barbecue sauce. Cook until the potatoes are browned and the chicken is warmed through, about 5 minutes. Season with salt and pepper and serve with salsa and sour cream.

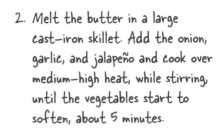

CHICKEN WITH COCONUT & CUCUMBER NOODLES

Yield: 4 Servings

Active Time: 30 Minutes / Total Time: 40 Minutes

The combination of warming cumin, sweet coconut, and crispy cucumber is endlessly satisfying when paired with succulent rotisserie chicken.

Ingredients

5 large cucumbers, peeled, halved lengthwise, and seeded

½ cup shredded unsweetened coconut

Zest and juice of 2 limes

¼ cup coconut milk

1 teaspoon chili garlic sauce, plus more as needed

½-inch piece fresh ginger, peeled and grated

1 teaspoon sugar

1 teaspoon cumin

1 teaspoon kosher salt, plus more to taste

3 cups shredded rotisserie chicken

½ cup roasted peanuts, chopped

6 scallions, trimmed and sliced thin

1. Quarter each cucumber half and then cut the quarters into 1/8-inch-wide "noodles." Place the strands on paper towels to drain.

2. Place the coconut, lime juice, coconut milk, chili garlic sauce, ginger, sugar, cumin, and salt in a blender and puree until smooth.

3. Place the cucumber noodles and chicken in a large serving bowl. Add the coconut mixture and toss to coat. Sprinkle the lime zest, peanuts, and scallions on top, season to taste, and serve immediately.

RICE BOWL WITH BENIHANA'S GINGER DRESSING

Yield: 4 Servings

Active Time: 30 Minutes / Total Time: 45 Minutes

The secret of the popular chain's famed dressing is out, and here it elevates what should be a humble bowl of rice.

Ingredients

For the Dressing

¼ cup chopped white onion

¼ cup peanut oil

1 tablespoon rice vinegar

1-inch piece fresh ginger, peeled and minced

1 tablespoon minced celery

1 tablespoon soy sauce

1 teaspoon tomato paste

1½ teaspoons sugar

1 teaspoon fresh lemon juice

½ teaspoon kosher salt

Black pepper, to taste

For the Rice Bowls

1 cup cooked white rice, at room temperature

1 cup canned adzuki beans, drained and rinsed

3 cups diced rotisserie chicken

1 carrot, peeled and grated

½ jicama, peeled and julienned

12 sugar snap peas, sliced

Flesh from 1 avocado, sliced thin

Salt, to taste

Sesame seeds, for garnish

1. To prepare the dressing, place all of the ingredients in a blender or food processor and puree until smooth.

2. To prepare the rice bowls, divide the rice between four bowls. Arrange the beans, chicken, carrot, jicama, snap peas, and avocado on top of each portion.

3. Top each portion with a pinch of salt and the dressing, garnish with the sesame seeds, and serve.

CHICKEN CONGEE

Yield: 4 Servings

Active Time: 10 Minutes / Total Time: 45 Minutes

This paragon of Chinese comfort food makes for a surprisingly wonderful breakfast.

Ingredients

4 cups chicken stock (see pages 92–93 for homemade)

2 tablespoons olive oil

1 garlic clove, minced

1½ cups long-grain rice

Salt and pepper, to taste

2 cups diced rotisserie chicken

1 teaspoon turmeric

Fresh cilantro, finely chopped, for garnish

1. Place the stock in a Dutch oven and bring to a simmer over medium heat.

2. Place the oil in a cast-iron wok or skillet and warm over medium heat. When the oil starts to shimmer, add the garlic and cook until it is fragrant and golden brown, about 2 minutes. Add the rice, stir until coated with the oil, and cook until the rice is golden brown, about 4 minutes.

3. Add the rice to the stock and season with salt and pepper. Cook, while stirring occasionally, until the rice is tender, about 20 minutes.

4. Stir the chicken and turmeric into the rice and cook until warmed through. Ladle into warmed bowls and garnish with cilantro.

CHICKEN FRIED RICE

Yield: 6 Servings

Active Time: 25 Minutes / Total Time: 35 Minutes

The next time you order Chinese food, add one or two sides of white rice. Alongside the rotisserie chicken, you're more than halfway home to another delicious meal.

Ingredients

¼ cup olive oil

1-inch piece fresh ginger, peeled and minced

2 garlic cloves, minced

3 large eggs

2 cups minced carrots

4 cups cooked, day-old white rice

4 scallions, trimmed and chopped

1 cup frozen peas

½ cup diced pineapple

2 tablespoons soy sauce

1 tablespoon rice vinegar

1 tablespoon fish sauce

1 tablespoon sesame oil

3 cups diced rotisserie chicken

1. Place the olive oil in a 12-inch cast-iron skillet and warm over medium-high heat. When the oil starts to shimmer, add the ginger and garlic and cook until they just start to brown, about 2 minutes.

2. Add the eggs and cook until they are set, about 2 minutes.

3. Add the carrots, rice, scallions, peas, and pineapple and stir to incorporate. Add the soy sauce, rice vinegar, fish sauce, and sesame oil and cook, while stirring constantly, for 5 minutes.

4. Add the chicken, stir to incorporate, and serve immediately.

PAD THAI

Yield: 4 to 6 Servings
Active Time: 15 Minutes / Total Time: 35 Minutes

The key here is balancing the flavors properly so that you have a tangle of chewy noodles freighted with a delicious jumble of salty, sweet, sour, and spicy.

Ingredients

6 oz. rice noodles

1 tablespoon olive oil

1 large egg

2 to 3 cups shredded rotisserie chicken

¼ cup tamarind paste

2 tablespoons water

1½ tablespoons fish sauce

2 tablespoons rice vinegar

1½ tablespoons brown sugar

4 scallions, trimmed and sliced

1 cup bean sprouts

½ teaspoon cayenne pepper

¼ cup crushed peanuts

Lime wedges, for serving

1. Place the noodles in a baking dish and cover with boiling water. Stir and let stand until tender, about 15 minutes.

2. Place the oil in a large wok or skillet and warm over medium—high heat. When the oil starts to shimmer, add the egg and cook until it is almost set, just over 1 minute.

3. Add the noodles and chicken and stir to incorporate. Add the tamarind paste, water, fish sauce, vinegar, brown sugar, scallions, bean sprouts, cayenne pepper, and peanuts. Stir to combine and cook until everything is warmed through, about 5 minutes. Serve with the lime wedges.

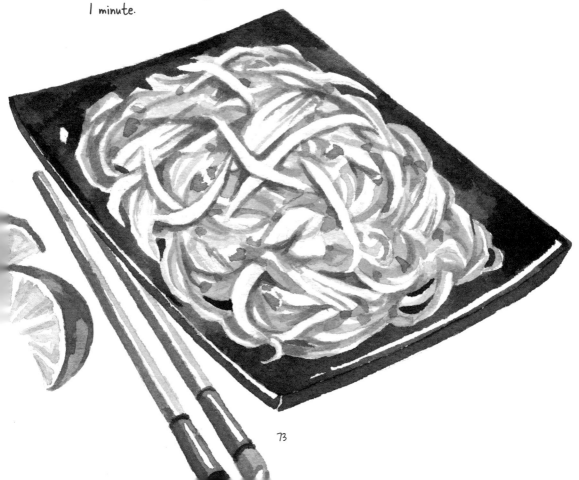

CHICKEN CURRY WITH BASMATI RICE

Yield: 4 to 6 Servings
Active Time: 20 Minutes / Total Time: 1 Hour

Pureeing spinach or basil leaves with the coconut milk before adding it to the pan is a great way to sneak additional flavor and nutrients into this curry.

Ingredients

5 tablespoons green curry paste

3 cups diced rotisserie chicken

2 tablespoons olive oil

2 yellow onions, peeled and sliced

2 red bell peppers, stemmed, seeded, and sliced

3-inch piece fresh ginger, peeled and mashed

1 garlic clove, mashed

3 tablespoons fish sauce

1 tablespoon Madras curry powder

1 (14 oz.) can coconut milk

2 tablespoons finely chopped fresh basil, plus more for garnish

1½ cups basmati rice

1 cup water

Lime wedges, for serving

Fresh cilantro, finely chopped, for garnish

1. Preheat the oven to 375°F. Place 2 tablespoons of the green curry paste and the chicken in a mixing bowl, stir until the chicken is evenly coated, and let stand for 15 minutes.

2. Place the oil in a 12-inch cast-iron skillet and warm over medium-high heat. When the oil starts to shimmer, add the onions, peppers, ginger, and garlic and cook, stirring frequently, until the vegetables start to soften, about 5 minutes.

3. Add the remaining green curry paste and cook until fragrant, about 4 minutes.

4. Add the fish sauce, curry powder, coconut milk, and basil and stir until combined. Stir in the rice and water and then place the chicken in the pan. Cover and transfer the pan to the oven. Bake until the rice is tender and has absorbed all of the liquid, about 25 minutes. Serve with the lime wedges and garnish with cilantro and additional basil.

CHICKEN LO MEIN

Yield: 4 to 6 Servings

Active Time: 45 Minutes / Total Time: 45 Minutes

Green or napa cabbage is preferred here, as red is just a bit too robust. Chopped bok choy is another good option if you're not the biggest cabbage fan.

Ingredients

2 teaspoons cornstarch

2 teaspoons water

5 tablespoons peanut oil

2 rotisserie chicken breasts, sliced thin

2 cups mung bean sprouts

½ lb. Chinese egg noodles

2 garlic cloves, minced

4 cups shredded cabbage

2 carrots, peeled and julienned

Salt, to taste

1 tablespoon Shaoxing rice wine

2½ tablespoons dark soy sauce

1 teaspoon toasted sesame oil

½ teaspoon sugar

4 scallions, trimmed and minced

1. Whisk the cornstarch, water, and ½ tablespoon of the peanut oil together in a mixing bowl. Add the chicken and toss until the chicken is evenly coated.

2. Bring water to a boil in a large saucepan. Add the bean sprouts and cook for 2 minutes. Remove them with a strainer, immediately run them under cold water, and let them drain.

3. Bring the water back to a boil, add the noodles, and cook until tender but still chewy, about 5 minutes. Drain and transfer to a medium bowl. Add ½ tablespoon of the peanut oil, toss to coat, and set aside.

4. Heat a wok or large skillet over medium heat for 2 to 3 minutes. Add 2 tablespoons of the peanut oil and raise the heat to medium–high. When the oil starts to shimmer, add the chicken and cook until golden brown, about 2 to 3 minutes. Transfer to a warmed plate and tent with aluminum foil to keep warm. Add the remaining peanut oil and the garlic to the pan, cook for 1 minute, and then add the cabbage, carrots, and a couple pinches of salt. Cook for 2 minutes, add the rice wine, and then stir in the noodles and chicken. Cook, while tossing, for 1 minute. Cover the pan and let steam for 1 minute.

5. Remove the lid and stir in the soy sauce, sesame oil, and sugar. Cook for 1 minute, add the bean sprouts and scallions, and cook, while stirring, for 1 minute. Serve immediately.

CASHEW BUTTER CHICKEN

Yield: 4 Servings

Active Time: 10 Minutes / Total Time: 20 Minutes

The cashew butter lends a rich and creamy quality that brings the best out of both the Swiss chard and the spicy chicken.

Ingredients

½ teaspoon kosher salt, plus more to taste

½ teaspoon cayenne pepper, plus more to taste

½ teaspoon brown sugar

½ teaspoon chili powder

3 cups shredded rotisserie chicken

⅓ cup cashew butter

¼ cup soy sauce

1½ tablespoons rice vinegar

2½ teaspoons toasted sesame oil

2 teaspoons chili oil

¾ teaspoon sugar

2 garlic cloves, minced

¾ lb. Chinese egg noodles

1 lb. Swiss chard, stems removed, leaves sliced into ribbons

6 scallions, trimmed and sliced thin

1. Place the salt, cayenne pepper, brown sugar, and chili powder in a mixing bowl and stir until well combined. Add the chicken and toss to coat.

2. Place the cashew butter, soy sauce, rice vinegar, sesame oil, chili oil, sugar, and garlic in a separate mixing bowl and stir until well combined.

3. Bring a large pot of salted water to a boil. Add the noodles and cook for 1 minute. Add the Swiss chard and cook until the noodles are tender but still chewy, another 2 to 3 minutes. Drain and transfer to a large bowl. Add the shredded chicken and the cashew butter mixture, toss to coat evenly, top with the scallions, and serve.

CHICKEN & EGGPLANT STIR-FRY

Yield: 4 Servings

Active Time: 35 Minutes / Total Time: 35 Minutes

Shaoxing rice wine's legendary ability to enhance the meaty flavor in any dish is on full display here, as both the chicken and eggplant shine from its inclusion.

Ingredients

4 lbs. eggplant, trimmed and peeled

2 tablespoons Shaoxing rice wine

1 tablespoon soy sauce

2 teaspoons toasted sesame oil

2 rotisserie chicken breasts, sliced thin

2 tablespoons peanut oil

2 jalapeño peppers, stemmed, seeded, and sliced thin

1 red bell pepper, stemmed, seeded, and sliced thin

2 garlic cloves, minced

2 scallions, trimmed and chopped

1. Cut each eggplant into ¼-inch-thick rounds, then cut each round into ¼-inch-wide strips.

2. Whisk the rice wine, soy sauce, and sesame oil together in a medium bowl. Add the chicken and toss until evenly coated.

3. Place the oil in a large wok or skillet and warm over medium-high heat for 2 to 3 minutes.

When the oil starts to shimmer, add the peppers and cook until they start to soften, about 3 minutes. Add the garlic and scallions and cook until they start to brown, about 2 minutes.

4. Add the chicken and eggplant to the pan and cook, while stirring, until everything is warmed through, about 4 minutes. Serve immediately.

CHICKEN PAELLA

Yield: 4 to 6 Servings

Active Time: 30 Minutes / Total Time: 45 Minutes

Purists see the saffron as key to this dish, but if you don't want to break the bank for this exceptionally precious material, turmeric makes for a fine substitute.

Ingredients

½ cup finely chopped fresh parsley

3 tablespoons olive oil

1 lemon, ½ juiced, ½ cut into wedges

Salt and pepper, to taste

3 cups diced or shredded rotisserie chicken

½ lb. chorizo

¼ cup diced pancetta

½ large white onion, chopped

1 bell pepper, stemmed, seeded, and chopped

4 garlic cloves, minced

1 cup chopped Roma tomatoes

3 cups short-grain rice

6 cups chicken stock (see pages 92–93 for homemade)

1 teaspoon saffron or turmeric

1 tablespoon pimentón

1 cup frozen peas

1. Preheat the oven to 450°F. Place 2 tablespoons of the parsley, 2 tablespoons of the olive oil, the lemon juice, salt, and pepper in a bowl and stir to combine. Add the chicken to the bowl and marinate for 15 minutes.

2. Place the remaining olive oil in a cast-iron skillet and warm over medium-high heat. When the oil starts to shimmer, place the chorizo, pancetta, onion, bell pepper, and half of the garlic in the skillet and cook until the onion is browned, about 10 minutes.

3. Season with salt and pepper and add the tomatoes, rice, stock, the remaining garlic and parsley, saffron or turmeric, and pimentón. Cook for 10 minutes, while stirring often.

4. Reduce the heat to medium-low and press the chicken into the mixture in the skillet. Cover the skillet and cook for 10 minutes.

5. Uncover the skillet and add the peas. Cover the skillet, place it in the oven, and bake until the rice is tender, about 12 minutes. Serve with the lemon wedges.

DRY-FRIED BEANS

Yield: 4 Servings

Active Time: 15 Minutes / Total Time: 25 Minutes

Keep your hands off the saltshaker when prepping this dish, as the soy sauce and fermented black bean garlic sauce will provide plenty.

Ingredients

1 tablespoon olive oil, plus more as needed

1 lb. green beans, trimmed

2 tablespoons sauerkraut or kimchi, chopped

1 garlic clove, chopped

2 tablespoons Shaoxing rice wine

1 to 2 cups shredded rotisserie chicken

2 tablespoons soy sauce

1 tablespoon fermented black bean garlic sauce

1 teaspoon sugar

Cooked white rice, for serving

1. Place the oil in a large skillet and warm over high heat. When the oil starts to shimmer, add the beans and let them sear on one side, undisturbed, for 6 minutes. Stir the beans and sear until they are well browned all over. Transfer to a bowl and set aside.

2. Add the sauerkraut or kimchi and the garlic to the pan. Cook, stirring continuously, until the contents of the pan are fragrant, about 2 minutes. Add more oil if the pan starts to look dry.

3. Add the rice wine and cook until it is nearly evaporated, about 4 minutes. Add the chicken, soy sauce, fermented black bean garlic sauce, and sugar and stir to incorporate. Return the green beans to the pan, cook until warmed through, and serve with white rice.

RISOTTO WITH CHICKEN & MUSHROOMS

Yield: 4 Servings

Active Time: 35 Minutes / Total Time: 35 Minutes

Don't be intimidated by risotto—a little attention and gumption is all this wonderful dish requires.

Ingredients

2 cups chicken stock (see pages 92–93 for homemade)

1 tablespoon unsalted butter

2 tablespoons olive oil

1 shallot, chopped

1 cup arborio rice

¼ cup dry white wine

Water, as needed

¼ cup grated fontina cheese, plus more for garnish

Salt and pepper, to taste

1 tablespoon fresh lemon juice, or to taste

4 oz oyster mushrooms, separated and trimmed

2 rotisserie chicken breasts, sliced

1. Place the stock in a small saucepan and bring to a simmer over medium heat. Turn off the heat and leave the pan on the stove.

2. Place the butter and half of the olive oil in a large skillet and warm over medium heat. Add the shallot and sauté until it just starts to brown, about 5 minutes. Add the rice and cook until it starts to give off a nutty fragrance, stirring constantly to ensure that it does not brown.

3. Deglaze the pan with the white wine and scrape up any browned bits from the bottom of the pan.

4. When the wine has been fully absorbed by the rice, add the warm stock a little at a time, stirring constantly to prevent sticking, and cook until the rice absorbs the stock. If the rice is still crunchy by the time you have used up all of the broth, add water in 1-tablespoon increments.

5. When the rice is al dente, stir in the cheese, season with salt and pepper, and add the lemon juice. Stir to incorporate and remove the skillet from heat.

6. Place remaining oil in a large sauté pan, warm over medium-high heat, and then add the mushrooms in one layer. Add a pinch of salt and cook until the mushrooms brown, about 5 minutes. Stir the mushrooms, add another pinch of salt, and cook until browned all over, another 5 minutes. Add the chicken, stir to combine, and cook until warmed through. Divide the risotto between four bowls and top with the mushroom-and-chicken mixture.

CHICKEN GUMBO

Yield: 4 Servings
Active Time: 25 Minutes / Total Time: 50 Minutes

Some would call this a soup, but it's better to think of it as a Cajun curry—and as one would expect, it's great with rice.

Ingredients

1 tablespoon olive oil

6 oz. Andouille sausage, chopped

1/3 cup all-purpose flour

1 onion, chopped

1 green bell pepper, stemmed, seeded, and chopped

3/4 cup chopped celery

1/2 tablespoon minced jalapeño pepper

2 scallions, trimmed and chopped

2 garlic cloves, minced

1/2 cup sliced okra

1 tomato, seeded and chopped

6 cups chicken stock (see pages 92–93 for homemade)

1 cup long-grain rice

1 bay leaf

1/4 teaspoon dried oregano

1/4 teaspoon onion powder

1/8 teaspoon dried thyme

1/8 teaspoon dried basil

2 cups shredded or diced rotisserie chicken

Salt and pepper, to taste

1. Preheat the oven to 375°F. Place the oil and sausage in a large saucepan and cook over medium heat, stirring occasionally, until the sausage starts to brown, about 5 minutes. Remove from heat.

2. Place the flour on a baking sheet, place it in the oven, and bake until the flour turns dark brown, 5 to 8 minutes. Remove and set aside.

3. Add the onion, green bell pepper, celery, jalapeño, scallions, garlic, okra, and tomato to the saucepan and cook until they are soft, about 10 minutes. Add the browned flour to the pan and cook, stirring constantly, for 4 minutes. Add the stock and stir to prevent any lumps from forming. Bring to a boil, reduce heat so that the soup simmers, and add the rice, bay leaf, oregano, onion powder, thyme, and basil. Cook until the rice is tender, about 25 minutes.

4. Stir in the chicken and season with salt and pepper. Cook until everything is warmed through, about 2 minutes, and then ladle into warmed bowls.

SOUPS

Of all the dishes chicken sits at the center of, it feels like soups are its true home. Nourishing, comforting, and restorative—the preparations here may take a little more time than a sandwich or a salad, but, considering all the time your rotisserie chicken has saved you, you're still way ahead.

CHICKEN STOCK

Yield: 8 Cups

Active Time: 20 Minutes / Total Time: 6 Hours

Shifting from store-bought to homemade stock is the easiest way to lift the dishes coming out of your kitchen.

Ingredients

3 rotisserie chicken carcasses, cleaned and rinsed

4 cups chopped yellow onions

2 cups chopped carrots

2 cups chopped celery

3 garlic cloves, crushed

3 sprigs fresh thyme

1 teaspoon black peppercorns

1 bay leaf

Salt, to taste

1. Place the chicken carcasses in a stockpot and cover with cold water. Bring to a simmer over medium–high heat and use a ladle to skim off any impurities that rise to the top. Add the vegetables, thyme, peppercorns, and bay leaf, season with salt, reduce the heat to low, and simmer for 5 hours, skimming occasionally to remove any impurities that rise to the top.

2. Strain, let cool slightly, and transfer to the refrigerator. Leave the stock uncovered and allow to cool completely. Remove the layer of fat from the top and cover. The stock will keep in the refrigerator for 3 to 5 days and in the freezer for up to 3 months.

CHICKEN NOODLE SOUP

Yield: 4 Servings

Active Time: 10 Minutes / Total Time: 40 Minutes

A giant step up from what comes in a can from Campbell's.

Ingredients

1 tablespoon olive oil

½ yellow onion, minced

1 carrot, peeled and minced

1 celery stalk, minced

1 tablespoon finely chopped fresh thyme

4 cups chicken stock (see pages 92–93 for homemade)

Salt and pepper, to taste

1½ cups egg noodles

2 to 3 cups diced rotisserie chicken

1. Place the oil in a large saucepan and warm over medium–high heat. When the oil starts to shimmer, add the onion and cook until it starts to soften, about 5 minutes. Add the carrot and celery and cook until they start to soften, about 5 minutes. Add the thyme and stock, bring to a boil, reduce the heat, and simmer for 20 minutes.

2. Season the soup with salt and pepper, add the egg noodles and the chicken, and cook until the noodles are al dente, about 7 minutes. Ladle into warmed bowls and serve.

BUTTERNUT SQUASH, QUINOA & CHICKEN SOUP

Yield: 4 Servings

Active Time: 20 Minutes / Total Time: 1 Hour and 10 Minutes

This is a great post-workout meal, thanks to the healthy carbs from the sweet potato, the nutrient-dense quinoa, and protein from the chicken. Plus, it just tastes good.

Ingredients

1 butternut squash, halved
and seeded

3 tablespoons olive oil

1 yellow onion, chopped

2 garlic cloves, minced

4 cups chicken stock (see
pages 92–93 for homemade)

1 (14 oz.) can stewed
tomatoes, chopped

Leaves from 1 sprig fresh
oregano, chopped

2 to 3 cups diced rotisserie chicken

2/3 cup quinoa, rinsed

Salt and pepper, to taste

1. Preheat the oven to 375°F.
   Place the butternut squash on a
   baking sheet, cut-side up, drizzle
   2 tablespoons of the oil over
   the top, and place in the oven.
   Roast for 40 minutes, or until
   the flesh is very tender. Remove
   from the oven and let cool.

2. Place the remaining oil in a large
   saucepan and warm over medium–
   high heat. When the oil starts
   to shimmer, add the onion and
   cook until it has softened, about
   5 minutes. Add the garlic, cook
   for 2 minutes, and then add 3
   cups of the stock, the stewed
   tomatoes, and the oregano.

3. Bring to a boil and then
   reduce the heat so that the
   soup simmers.

4. Scoop the flesh of the
   butternut squash into a food
   processor or blender with the
   remaining stock. Puree until
   smooth.

5. Add the butternut squash
   puree, chicken, and quinoa to
   the simmering broth. Cook until
   the quinoa is tender, about 15
   minutes.

6. Season with salt and pepper and
   ladle into warmed bowls.

SOUTHWESTERN CORN CHOWDER

Yield: 4 Servings

Active Time: 15 Minutes / Total Time: 40 Minutes

Chunks of chicken in a creamy, piquant broth makes a bowl of this the antidote for the winter blues.

Ingredients

1 tablespoon olive oil

1 large onion, peeled and minced

2 garlic cloves, peeled and minced

3 corn tortillas

1 cup chopped tomatoes

½ jalapeño pepper, stemmed, seeded, and minced (optional)

4 cups chicken stock (see pages 92–93 for homemade)

1 teaspoon cumin

1 teaspoon coriander

1 teaspoon dried oregano

1 teaspoon ancho chile powder

2 cups chopped rotisserie chicken

1½ cups frozen corn

1 red bell pepper, stemmed, seeded, and chopped

½ cup heavy cream

Salt and pepper, to taste

Lime wedges, for serving

Tortilla chips, for serving

1. Place the oil in a large saucepan and warm over medium heat. Add the onion and garlic and cook until the onion turns translucent, about 3 minutes.

2. Slice the tortillas into strips and add them to the pot. Cook, stirring occasionally, until they start to brown, about 5 minutes.

3. Add the tomatoes, jalapeño (if using), stock, cumin, coriander, oregano, and ancho chile powder and bring to a boil. Reduce the heat so that the soup simmers and cook for 10 minutes.

4. Remove from heat and let cool for 5 minutes. Use a food processor or blender to puree the soup. Return the soup to the pan. Add the chicken, corn, bell pepper, and cream. Warm over medium heat until the corn is thawed and cooked through, about 5 minutes.

5. Season with salt and pepper, ladle into warmed bowls, and serve with the lime wedges and tortilla chips.

CORN & RED PEPPER BISQUE WITH BUTTER-POACHED CHICKEN

Yield: 4 Servings

Active Time: 30 Minutes / Total Time: 1 Hour and 30 Minutes

Poaching the chicken in butter adds so much richness and tenderness that you'll hardly believe it's the same bird you carried home from the store.

Ingredients

3 cups corn kernels

2 tablespoons olive oil

Salt and pepper, to taste

3 red bell peppers

1½ sticks unsalted butter

½ cup heavy cream

½ cup milk

2 cups diced rotisserie chicken

1. Preheat the oven to 375°F. Place the corn in a single layer on a large baking sheet and drizzle the oil over it. Season with salt, place in the oven, and roast until the corn starts to darken and caramelize, 12 to 18 minutes. Remove from the oven and raise the temperature to 425°F.

2. Place the peppers on a baking sheet and place them in the oven. Roast, while turning occasionally, until the skins are blistered all over, about 30 minutes. Remove from the oven and let cool. When cool enough to handle, remove the skins and seeds and discard. Set the peppers aside.

3. Place the corn, peppers, ½ stick of the butter, cream, and milk in a saucepan and bring to a simmer, while stirring, over medium heat. Simmer for 20 minutes, stirring often to make sure the bisque does not come to a boil.

4. While the bisque is simmering, place the remaining butter in a small saucepan and melt over low heat. Add the chicken and poach for 7 to 10 minutes, spooning the butter over the chicken. When the chicken is very tender and warmed through, remove from heat and set aside.

5. After simmering for 20 minutes, remove the bisque from heat and let cool for 10 minutes. Transfer the bisque to a blender or food processor and puree until smooth. If the mixture has cooled too much, return to the saucepan and cook until warmed through. If not, ladle into warmed bowls and top each portion with some of the poached chicken.

CHICKEN CHILI

Yield: 4 to 6 Servings
Active Time: 10 Minutes / Total Time: 30 Minutes

If you're looking for a little more flavor here, try stirring in about a tablespoon of spicy mustard when you add the canned beans.

Ingredients

1 tablespoon olive oil

1 yellow onion, chopped

2 garlic cloves, minced

1 tablespoon chili powder

1 bay leaf

2 sprigs fresh thyme

2 sprigs fresh parsley

4 cups diced or shredded rotisserie chicken

4 tomatoes, diced

2 cups tomato sauce

½ cup tomato paste

1 (14 oz.) can kidney beans

1 (14 oz.) can cannellini beans

1 (14 oz.) can black beans

Salt and pepper, to taste

Cheddar cheese, shredded, for serving

Sour cream, for serving

Fresh chives, finely chopped, for serving

1. Place the oil in a large saucepan and warm over medium—high heat. When the oil starts to shimmer, add the onion and cook until it starts to soften, about 5 minutes.

2. Add the garlic and cook until it just starts to brown, about 2 minutes. Add the remaining ingredients, except for those designated for serving, and stir to combine. Bring to a boil, reduce heat so that the chili simmers, and cook until the chili has thickened and the taste is to your liking, about 20 minutes.

3. Season with salt and pepper, remove the aromatics and discard, and ladle the chili into warmed bowls. Serve with the cheddar cheese, sour cream, and chives.

CHICKEN CHILI VERDE

Yield: 4 to 6 Servings

Active Time: 15 Minutes / Total Time: 50 Minutes

As this chili is traditionally made with pork shoulder, it's a good place to utilize the darker meat from the chicken's thighs, legs, and wings.

Ingredients

1 jalapeño pepper

1 tablespoon olive oil

1 onion, chopped

2 garlic cloves, minced

1 (14 oz.) can fire-roasted tomatoes

2 tomatillos, husked, rinsed, and chopped

4 cups chicken stock (see pages 92–93 for homemade)

1 teaspoon finely chopped fresh oregano

3 cups diced rotisserie chicken

Pinch of ground cloves

Salt and pepper, to taste

Cooked white rice, for serving

1. Using metal tongs, hold the jalapeño over an open flame until it is charred all over. Place in a heatproof bowl, cover with a kitchen towel, and let stand for 5 minutes.

2. Remove the stem and seeds from the jalapeño and discard them. Chop the remaining jalapeño and reserve for garnish.

3. Place the olive oil in a large saucepan and warm over medium-high heat. When the oil starts to shimmer, add the onion and garlic and cook until the onion starts to soften, about 5 minutes. Add the tomatoes, tomatillos, stock, oregano, chicken, and cloves. Bring to a boil, reduce heat to low, cover, and cook for 20 minutes, stirring occasionally.

4. Remove 2 cups of the broth, taking care not to remove any of the chicken, and place it in a food processor. Puree until smooth. Return the puree to the saucepan and cook for 25 minutes, while stirring occasionally.

5. Season with salt and pepper, garnish with the reserved jalapeño, and serve with white rice.

CARIBBEAN CHICKEN SOUP

Yield: 4 Servings

Active Time: 15 Minutes / Total Time: 30 Minutes

This recipe is steeped in the rich Afro-Caribbean culinary tradition. Make sure you don't skip the lime wedges—that little touch of acid really ties the dish together.

Ingredients

1 cup peanuts, chopped

10 okra pods, trimmed and sliced

½ cup coconut oil

1 red bell pepper, stemmed, seeded, and diced

1 yellow onion, sliced into half-moons

1 habanero pepper, stemmed, seeded, and diced

1 large potato, peeled and diced

4 cups chicken stock (see pages 92–93 for homemade)

1 cup clam juice

1 cup coconut milk

Salt, to taste

4 cups spinach

3 cups shredded rotisserie chicken

Lime wedges, for serving

1. Place the peanuts in a large, dry skillet and toast over medium heat until they start to brown, about 5 minutes. Remove them from the pan and set aside. Add the okra and cook, while stirring, until it is browned all over, about 5 minutes. Remove and set aside.

2. Place the coconut oil in a large saucepan and warm over medium heat. When it starts to shimmer, add the bell pepper, onion, habanero pepper, and potato and cook until the onion starts to soften, about 5 minutes.

3. Add the stock and clam juice, bring to a simmer, and cook until the potato is tender, about 8 minutes. Add the coconut milk, return to a simmer, and season with salt.

4. Working in batches, transfer the soup to a blender and puree until smooth. Return the soup to the Dutch oven and simmer for another 5 minutes. Stir in the peanuts, okra, spinach, and chicken and cook until the spinach has wilted, 2 to 3 minutes. Ladle the soup into warmed bowls and serve with lime wedges.

CHICKEN DUMPLINGS

Yield: 18 Dumplings
Active Time: 5 Minutes / Total Time: 20 Minutes

As a side or in a broth, these dumplings bring a whole new realm of comfort within reach.

Ingredients

4 slices of bread, chopped

½ cup finely chopped fresh parsley

1¼ cups all-purpose flour

1 teaspoon baking powder

½ cup whole milk

1 egg

4 tablespoons unsalted butter, melted

1 cup minced rotisserie chicken

Salt and pepper, to taste

4 cups chicken stock (see pages 92–93 for homemade)

1. Place the bread and parsley in a food processor and pulse until combined. Add the flour and baking powder and blitz to incorporate. With the food processor running on low, gradually incorporate the milk, egg, and butter.

2. Add the chicken to the work bowl and fold to incorporate. Season with salt and pepper and then set the mixture aside.

3. Place the stock in a saucepan and bring to a boil over medium–high heat. Drop tablespoons of the dumpling mixture into the stock, cover, and cook for 12 minutes. Serve the dumplings in the broth, or drain and serve the dumplings as a side.

AVGOLEMONO

Yield: 4 Servings

Active Time: 15 Minutes / Total Time: 25 Minutes

Avgolemono means "egg and lemon," and these two ingredients combine to produce a nourishing soup that is one of the most popular dishes in Greek cuisine.

Ingredients

6 cups chicken stock (see pages 92–93 for homemade)

½ cup orzo

3 eggs

1 tablespoon fresh lemon juice

1 tablespoon cold water

1½ cups diced rotisserie chicken

Salt and pepper, to taste

Lemon slices, for garnish

Fresh parsley, finely chopped, for garnish

1. Place the stock in a large saucepan and bring to a boil. Reduce heat so that the stock simmers, add the orzo, and cook for 5 minutes.

2. Strain the stock and orzo over a large bowl. Set the orzo aside. Return the stock to the pan and bring to a simmer.

3. Place the eggs in a mixing bowl and beat until scrambled. Add the lemon juice and cold water and whisk to incorporate. While stirring constantly, add approximately ½ cup of the stock to the mixture. Stir another cup of stock into the egg mixture and then stir the tempered eggs into the saucepan. Be careful not to let the stock come to boil once you add the tempered eggs.

4. Stir the chicken and orzo into the soup and cook until warmed through, about 2 minutes. Season with salt and pepper, ladle into warmed bowls, and garnish with the lemon slices and parsley.

AFRICAN PEANUT SOUP

Yield: 4 to 6 Servings

Active Time: 25 Minutes / Total Time: 50 Minutes

A dish so good you can feel comfortable pulling it out for company.

Ingredients

½ cup smooth peanut butter

2 tablespoons tomato paste

6 cups chicken stock (see pages 92–93 for homemade)

1 onion, chopped

1-inch piece fresh ginger, peeled and minced

2 tablespoons finely chopped fresh thyme

1 bay leaf

1/8 teaspoon cayenne pepper, or to taste

1 sweet potato, peeled and chopped

2 cups diced rotisserie chicken

6 fresh okra, sliced

Salt and pepper, to taste

1. Place the peanut butter and tomato paste in a large saucepan and warm over medium heat. When the mixture starts to liquefy, gradually add the chicken stock, whisking constantly to keep lumps from forming.

2. Add the onion, ginger, thyme, bay leaf, and cayenne pepper and bring to a simmer. Cook for 30 minutes, stirring frequently.

3. Add the sweet potato and cook until it starts to soften, about 10 minutes. Add the chicken and okra and cook until the okra and sweet potato are tender, about 5 minutes. Season with salt and pepper and ladle into warmed bowls.

CHICKEN SUCCOTASH SOUP

Yield: 4 to 6 Servings
Active Time: 15 Minutes / Total Time: 25 Minutes

This soup is based on a classic Southern recipe, and the addition of chicken complements the sweetness of the corn beautifully.

Ingredients

4 tablespoons unsalted butter

4 slices of thick-cut bacon, chopped

2 onions, chopped

2 garlic cloves, minced

¼ cup all-purpose flour

4 cups chicken stock (see pages 92–93 for homemade)

2 to 3 cups diced rotisserie chicken

2 cups corn kernels

1 (14 oz.) can kidney beans, rinsed and drained

1 cup heavy cream

3 tablespoons finely chopped fresh parsley

Salt and pepper, to taste

1. Place the butter in a large saucepan and melt over medium heat. Add the bacon, onions, and garlic and cook until the bacon starts to brown and the onions start to soften, about 5 minutes.

2. Add the flour and cook, stirring constantly, for 3 minutes. Gradually add the stock and whisk constantly to prevent lumps from forming. Bring to a boil and then reduce heat so that the soup simmers. Add the chicken, corn kernels, and kidney beans and simmer for 5 minutes.

3. Add the cream and return to a simmer. Stir in the chopped parsley, season with salt and pepper, and ladle into warmed bowls.

CHICKEN MULLIGATAWNY

Yield: 4 to 6 Servings

Active Time: 15 Minutes / Total Time: 40 Minutes

Whip this up and enjoy a bowl with the "Soup Nazi" episode of *Seinfeld*—you'll understand just what Kramer and the rest of the gang are so excited about.

Ingredients

4 tablespoons unsalted butter

1 onion, chopped

2 carrots, peeled and chopped

2 celery stalks, chopped

2 tablespoons all-purpose flour

1 tablespoon curry powder

1 tablespoon poppy seeds

1 teaspoon cumin

4 cups chicken stock (see pages 92–93 for homemade)

⅓ cup long-grain rice

1 apple, peeled, cored, and chopped

1 to 2 cups diced rotisserie chicken

¼ teaspoon dried thyme

½ cup heavy cream

Salt and pepper, to taste

Fresh cilantro, finely chopped, for garnish

Cashews, chopped, for garnish

1. Place the butter in a large saucepan and melt over medium heat. Add the onion, carrots, and celery and sauté until the vegetables start to soften, about 5 minutes.

2. Stir in the flour, curry powder, poppy seeds, and cumin and cook until fragrant, about 3 minutes. Pour in the chicken stock and bring to a boil. Add the rice, reduce the heat so that the soup simmers, and cook for 15 minutes.

3. Add the apple, chicken, and thyme and simmer for another 10 minutes. Stir in the cream and bring the soup back to a simmer. Season with salt and pepper, ladle into warmed bowls, and garnish with the cilantro and cashews.

METRIC EQUIVALENTS

Weights

1 oz.	28 grams
2 oz.	57 grams
4 oz. (¼ lb.)	113 grams
8 oz. (½ lb.)	227 grams
16 oz. (1 lb.)	454 grams

Volume Measures

⅛ teaspoon		0.6 ml
¼ teaspoon		1.23 ml
½ teaspoon		2.5 ml
1 teaspoon		5 ml
1 tablespoon (3 teaspoons)	0.5 fluid oz.	15 ml
2 tablespoons	1 fluid oz.	29.5 ml
¼ cup (4 tablespoons)	2 fluid oz.	59 ml
⅓ cup (5⅓ tablespoons)	2.7 fluid oz.	80 ml
½ cup (8 tablespoons)	4 fluid oz.	120 ml
⅔ cup (10⅔ tablespoons)	5.4 fluid oz.	160 ml
¾ cup (12 tablespoons)	6 fluid oz.	180 ml
1 cup (16 tablespoons)	8 fluid oz.	240 ml

Temperature Equivalents

°F	°C	Gas Mark
225	110	1/4
250	130	1/2
275	140	1
300	150	2
325	170	3
350	180	4
375	190	5
400	200	6
425	220	7
450	230	8
475	240	9
500	250	10

Length Measures

1/16 inch	1.6 mm
1/8 inch	3 mm
1/4 inch	0.63 cm
1/2 inch	1.25 cm
3/4 inch	2 cm
1 inch	2.5 cm

INDEX

adzuki beans, Rice Bowl with Benihana's
   Ginger Dressing, 66–67
African Peanut Soup, 112–113
Aioli, Sun-Dried Tomato, 18–19
anchovy fillets, Chicken Caesar Salad,
   44–45
Andouille sausage, Chicken Gumbo, 88–89
apples
   Chicken Mulligatawny, 116–117
   Curried Chicken Salad, 48–49
arugula, Curried Chicken Salad, 48–49
asparagus
   Buddha Sesame Chicken, 60–61
   Chicken Ramen, 54–55
Avgolemono, 110–111
avocado, Rice Bowl with Benihana's Ginger
   Dressing, 66–67

bacon
   Chicken Paninis with Sun-Dried Tomato
     Aioli, 18–19
   Chicken Succotash Soup, 114–115
barbecue sauce
   BBQ Chicken Hash, 62–63
   BBQ Chicken Pizza, 38–39
   BBQ Chicken Sandwiches, 16–17
basil, Rice Noodle Salad, 46–47
Basmati Rice, Chicken Curry with, 74–75
BBQ Chicken Hash, 62–63

BBQ Chicken Pizza, 38–39
BBQ Chicken Sandwiches, 16–17
bean sprouts, Pad Thai, 72–73
beans
   Chicken Burritos, 20–21
   Chicken Chili, 102–103
   Chicken Succotash Soup, 114–115
   Dry-Fried Beans, 84–85
   Puerto Rican Rice & Beans, 58–59
   Rice Bowl with Benihana's Ginger
     Dressing, 66–67
   See also green beans
black beans
   Chicken Burritos, 20–21
   Chicken Chili, 102–103
bok choy, Chicken Ramen, 54–55
Buddha Sesame Chicken, 60–61
Burritos, Chicken, 20–21
Butternut Squash, Quinoa & Chicken Soup,
   96–97

cabbage
   Chicken Lo Mein, 76–77
   Chicken Tostadas with Cilantro-Lime
     Sour Cream, 26–27
Calzones, Chicken Parmesan, 36–37
cannellini beans, Chicken Chili, 102–103
Caribbean Chicken Soup, 106–107
carrots

Chicken Fried Rice, 70–71
Chicken Lo Mein, 76–77
Chicken Mulligatawny, 116–117
Chicken Noodle Soup, 94–95
Chicken Pot Pie, 40–41
Chicken Stock, 92–93
Rice Bowl with Benihana's Ginger
    Dressing, 66–67
Rice Noodle Salad, 46–47
Cashew Butter Chicken, 78–79
Casserole, Chicken & Tomatillo, 30–31
Cauliflower & Chickpea Salad, 50–51
celery
    Chicken Gumbo, 88–89
    Chicken Mulligatawny, 116–117
    Chicken Noodle Soup, 94–95
    Chicken Stock, 92–93
    Curried Chicken Salad, 48–49
cheddar cheese
    Chicken Chili, 102–103
    Chicken Paninis with Sun-Dried Tomato
        Aioli, 18–19
cheese. See individual types
Chicken & Eggplant Stir-Fry, 80–81
Chicken & Kimchi Pot Stickers, 32–33
Chicken & Mushroom Crepes, 34–35
Chicken & Tomatillo Casserole, 30–31
Chicken Burritos, 20–21
Chicken Caesar Salad, 44–45
Chicken Chili, 102–103
Chicken Chili Verde, 104–105

Chicken Congee, 68–69
Chicken Curry with Basmati Rice, 74–75
Chicken Dumplings, 108–109
Chicken Fajitas, 22–23
Chicken Fried Rice, 70–71
Chicken Gumbo, 88–89
Chicken Lo Mein, 76–77
Chicken Mulligatawny, 116–117
Chicken Paella, 82–83
Chicken Paninis with Sun-Dried Tomato Aioli,
    18–19
Chicken Parmesan Calzones, 36–37
Chicken Pot Pie, 40–41
Chicken Ramen, 54–55
Chicken Succotash Soup, 114–115
Chicken Tacos, 24–25
Chicken Tostadas with Cilantro-Lime Sour
    Cream, 26–27
Chicken with Coconut & Cucumber Noodles,
    64–65
Chickpea Salad, Cauliflower &, 50–51
chili
    Chicken Chili, 102–103
    Chicken Chili Verde, 104–105
chilies, green, Chipotle Chicken Enchiladas,
    28–29
Chipotle Chicken Enchiladas, 28–29
chorizo, Chicken Paella, 82–83
Chowder, Southwestern Corn, 98–99
cilantro
    Chicken Burritos, 20–21

Chicken Fajitas, 22–23
Chicken Tacos, 24–25
Chicken Tostadas with Cilantro–Lime
    Sour Cream, 26–27
Larb Gai, 52–53
Rice Noodle Salad, 46–47
Classic Chicken Salad Sandwiches, 12–13
coconut, Chicken with Coconut & Cucumber
  Noodles, 64–65
coconut milk
    Caribbean Chicken Soup, 106–107
    Chicken Curry with Basmati Rice, 74–75
    Chicken with Coconut & Cucumber
      Noodles, 64–65
corn
    Chicken Burritos, 20–21
    Chicken Succotash Soup, 114–115
    Chicken Tostadas with Cilantro–Lime
      Sour Cream, 26–27
    Corn & Red Pepper Bisque with Butter–
      Poached Chicken, 100–101
    Southwestern Corn Chowder, 98–99
Cotija cheese
    Chicken & Tomatillo Casserole, 30–31
    Chipotle Chicken Enchiladas, 28–29
Crepes, Chicken & Mushroom, 34–35
cucumber
    Chicken with Coconut & Cucumber
      Noodles, 64–65
    Garden Sesame Noodles, 56–57
Curried Chicken Salad, 48–49

Dry-Fried Beans, 84–85
Dumplings, Chicken, 108–109

Eggplant Stir-Fry, Chicken &, 80–81
eggs
    Chicken Fried Rice, 70–71
    Pad Thai, 72–73
Enchiladas, Chipotle Chicken, 28–29

Fajitas, Chicken, 22–23
fontina cheese, Risotto with Chicken &
  Mushrooms, 86–87

Garden Sesame Noodles, 56–57
ginger, fresh
    African Peanut Soup, 112–113
    Chicken & Kimchi Pot Stickers, 32–33
    Chicken Curry with Basmati Rice, 74–75
    Chicken Fried Rice, 70–71
    Chicken Ramen, 54–55
    Chicken with Coconut & Cucumber
      Noodles, 64–65
    Garden Sesame Noodles, 56–57
    Rice Bowl with Benihana's Ginger
      Dressing, 66–67
    Rice Noodle Salad, 46–47
gouda cheese, smoked, BBQ Chicken Pizza,
  38–39
green beans
    Chicken Pot Pie, 40–41
    Dry-Fried Beans, 84–85

Hash, BBQ Chicken, 62–63

jicama, Rice Bowl with Benihana's Ginger Dressing, 66–67

kidney beans
    Chicken Chili, 102–103
    Chicken Succotash Soup, 114–115
    Puerto Rican Rice & Beans, 58–59
kimchi
    Chicken & Kimchi Pot Stickers, 32–33
    Dry-Fried Beans, 84–85

Larb Gai, 52–53
lemongrass stalk, Larb Gai, 52–53
lettuce
    Chicken Caesar Salad, 44–45
    Larb Gai, 52–53
Lime Sour Cream, Chicken Tostadas with Cilantro–, 26–27
Lo Mein, Chicken, 76–77

marinara sauce
    Chicken Parmesan Calzones, 36–37
    See also tomato sauce
metric equivalents, 118–119
mozzarella cheese
    BBQ Chicken Pizza, 38–39
    Chicken Parmesan Calzones, 36–37
mung bean sprouts, Chicken Lo Mein, 76–77
mushrooms
    Buddha Sesame Chicken, 60–61
    Chicken & Mushroom Crepes, 34–35
    Chicken Ramen, 54–55

    Risotto with Chicken & Mushrooms, 86–87
noodles. See pasta and noodles

okra
    African Peanut Soup, 112–113
    Caribbean Chicken Soup, 106–107
    Chicken Gumbo, 88–89
olives, Puerto Rican Rice & Beans, 58–59
onions
    Chicken Curry with Basmati Rice, 74–75
    Chicken Stock, 92–93
    Chicken Succotash Soup, 114–115
orzo, Avgolemono, 110–111

Pad Thai, 72–73
pancetta, Chicken Paella, 82–83
Paninis with Sun-Dried Tomato Aioli, Chicken, 18–19
Parmesan cheese
    Chicken Caesar Salad, 44–45
    Chicken Parmesan Calzones, 36–37
pasta and noodles
    Avgolemono, 110–111
    Cashew Butter Chicken, 78–79
    Chicken Lo Mein, 76–77
    Chicken Noodle Soup, 94–95
    Chicken Ramen, 54–55
    Chicken with Coconut & Cucumber Noodles, 64–65
    Garden Sesame Noodles, 56–57
    Pad Thai, 72–73

Rice Noodle Salad, 46–47

PB & C Sandwiches, 14–15

peanut butter

Garden Sesame Noodles, 56–57

PB & C Sandwiches, 14–15

Peanut Sauce, 46–47

Rice Noodle Salad, 46–47

Peanut Sauce, 46–47

peanuts

African Peanut Soup, 112–113

Caribbean Chicken Soup, 106–107

Chicken with Coconut & Cucumber
Noodles, 64–65

Garden Sesame Noodles, 56–57

Pad Thai, 72–73

peas

Chicken Fried Rice, 70–71

Chicken Paella, 82–83

Garden Sesame Noodles, 56–57

Rice Bowl with Benihana's Ginger
Dressing, 66–67

pecans, Curried Chicken Salad, 48–49

pepper jack cheese, Chicken Burritos, 20–21

peppers, hot

BBQ Chicken Hash, 62–63

Caribbean Chicken Soup, 106–107

Cauliflower & Chickpea Salad, 50–51

Chicken & Eggplant Stir-Fry, 80–81

Chicken & Tomatillo Casserole, 30–31

Chicken Chili Verde, 104–105

Chicken Fajitas, 22–23

Chicken Gumbo, 88–89

Chicken Tacos, 24–25

Chicken Tostadas with Cilantro-Lime
Sour Cream, 26–27

Chipotle Chicken Enchiladas, 28–29

Larb Gai, 52–53

Rice Noodle Salad, 46–47

Southwestern Corn Chowder, 98–99

peppers, sweet

Caribbean Chicken Soup, 106–107

Chicken & Eggplant Stir-Fry, 80–81

Chicken Curry with Basmati Rice, 74–75

Chicken Fajitas, 22–23

Chicken Gumbo, 88–89

Chicken Paella, 82–83

Corn & Red Pepper Bisque with Butter-
Poached Chicken, 100–101

Curried Chicken Salad, 48–49

Garden Sesame Noodles, 56–57

Rice Noodle Salad, 46–47

Southwestern Corn Chowder, 98–99

piecrusts, Chicken Pot Pie, 40–41

pineapple, Chicken Fried Rice, 70–71

Pizza, BBQ Chicken, 38–39

Pot Pie, Chicken, 40–41

Pot Stickers, Chicken & Kimchi, 32–33

potatoes

BBQ Chicken Hash, 62–63

Caribbean Chicken Soup, 106–107

Chipotle Chicken Enchiladas, 28–29

Puerto Rican Rice & Beans, 58–59

quinoa, Butternut Squash, Quinoa & Chicken
Soup, 96–97

radishes, Chicken Ramen, 54–55
rice
  Chicken Burritos, 20–21
  Chicken Chili Verde, 104–105
  Chicken Congee, 68–69
  Chicken Curry with Basmati Rice, 74–75
  Chicken Fried Rice, 70–71
  Chicken Gumbo, 88–89
  Chicken Mulligatawny, 116–117
  Chicken Paella, 82–83
  Dry-Fried Beans, 84–85
  Puerto Rican Rice & Beans, 58–59
  Rice Bowl with Benihana's Ginger
    Dressing, 66–67
  Risotto with Chicken & Mushrooms,
    86–87
Rice Noodle Salad, 46–47
Risotto with Chicken & Mushrooms, 86–87

salads
  Cauliflower & Chickpea Salad, 50–51
  Chicken Caesar Salad, 44–45
  Classic Chicken Salad Sandwiches, 12–13
  Curried Chicken Salad, 48–49
  Larb Gai, 52–53
  Rice Noodle Salad, 46–47
salsa verde, Chicken & Tomatillo Casserole,
  30–31
sandwiches

BBQ Chicken Sandwiches, 16–17
Chicken Paninis with Sun-Dried Tomato
  Aioli, 18–19
Classic Chicken Salad Sandwiches, 12–13
PB & C Sandwiches, 14–15
sauerkraut, Dry-Fried Beans, 84–85
sausage
  Chicken Gumbo, 88–89
  Chicken Paella, 82–83
Sazón, Puerto Rican Rice & Beans, 58–59
scallions
  Cashew Butter Chicken, 78–79
  Cauliflower & Chickpea Salad, 50–51
  Chicken & Eggplant Stir-Fry, 80–81
  Chicken Fried Rice, 70–71
  Chicken Gumbo, 88–89
  Chicken Lo Mein, 76–77
  Chicken Paninis with Sun-Dried Tomato
    Aioli, 18–19
  Chicken with Coconut & Cucumber
    Noodles, 64–65
  Garden Sesame Noodles, 56–57
  Pad Thai, 72–73
  Rice Noodle Salad, 46–47
soups
  African Peanut Soup, 112–113
  Avgolemono, 110–111
  Butternut Squash, Quinoa & Chicken
    Soup, 96–97
  Caribbean Chicken Soup, 106–107
  Chicken Chili, 102–103

Chicken Chili Verde, 104–105
Chicken Congee, 68–69
Chicken Mulligatawny, 116–117
Chicken Noodle Soup, 94–95
Chicken Ramen, 54–55
Chicken Stock, 92–93
Chicken Succotash Soup, 114–115
Corn & Red Pepper Bisque with Butter-
     Poached Chicken, 100–101
Southwestern Corn Chowder, 98–99
Sour Cream, Cilantro-Lime, 26–27
Southwestern Corn Chowder, 98–99
spinach, Caribbean Chicken Soup, 106–107
squash, summer, Chicken Burritos, 20–21
squash, winter, Butternut Squash, Quinoa &
     Chicken Soup, 96–97
Stir-Fry, Chicken & Eggplant, 80–81
Sun-Dried Tomato Aioli, Chicken Paninis
     with, 18–19
sweet potato, African Peanut Soup, 112–113
Swiss chard, Cashew Butter Chicken, 78–79

Tacos, Chicken, 24–25
tahini, Garden Sesame Noodles, 56–57
tomatillos
     Chicken & Tomatillo Casserole, 30–31
     Chicken Chili Verde, 104–105
tomato sauce
     Chicken Chili, 102–103
     Chicken Parmesan Calzones, 36–37
     Puerto Rican Rice & Beans, 58–59
tomatoes

Butternut Squash, Quinoa & Chicken
     Soup, 96–97
Chicken & Tomatillo Casserole, 30–31
Chicken Chili, 102–103
Chicken Chili Verde, 104–105
Chicken Gumbo, 88–89
Chicken Paella, 82–83
Chicken Tacos, 24–25
Chicken Tostadas with Cilantro-Lime
     Sour Cream, 26–27
Chipotle Chicken Enchiladas, 28–29
Southwestern Corn Chowder, 98–99
tortillas
     Chicken & Tomatillo Casserole, 30–31
     Chicken Burritos, 20–21
     Chicken Fajitas, 22–23
     Chicken Tacos, 24–25
     Chicken Tostadas with Cilantro-Lime
         Sour Cream, 26–27
     Chipotle Chicken Enchiladas, 28–29
     Southwestern Corn Chowder, 98–99
Tostadas with Cilantro-Lime Sour Cream,
     Chicken, 26–27

wonton wrappers, Chicken & Kimchi Pot
     Stickers, 32–33

zucchini, Chicken Burritos, 20–21

ABOUT THE ILLUSTRATOR

Michelle Xu is an illustrator from New Jersey and an alumnus of the Rhode Island School of Design. She enjoys illustrating food just as much as she likes eating it.

ABOUT CIDER MILL PRESS
BOOK PUBLISHERS

Good ideas ripen with time. From seed to harvest, Cider Mill Press brings fine reading, information, and entertainment together between the covers of its creatively crafted books. Our Cider Mill bears fruit twice a year, publishing a new crop of titles each spring and fall.

"Where Good Books Are Ready for Press"

Visit us online at
cidermillpress.com
or write to us at
PO Box 454
12 Spring St.
Kennebunkport, Maine 04046